CONTENTS

KID'S socks

Paul Amato

SIZE
One size. Sized for child.

GAUGE
32 sts and 40 rows to 4"/10cm over St st in the round and stripe pattern.
Take time to check your gauge.

SPECIAL TECHNIQUE
To knit in the round with 2 circular needles
Divide sts on 2 needles as directed, join (being sure cast-on is not twisted), and use each needle to knit its own sts. When first needle is finished, its sts are slid to the middle (wire) section of the needle, and the circle of needles rotates clockwise. The yarn passes counter-clockwise from 1st needle to the 2nd needle, which then knits its own sts. The 2nd needle rests with its sts in the middle and passes the yarn to the 1st needle—one needle is at work while the other rests.

SHORT ROW WRAP & TURN (w&t)
On RS row (on WS row)
1 Wyib (wyif), sl next st purlwise.
2 Move yarn between the needles to the front (back).
3 Sl the same st to LH needle. Turn work. One st wrapped.
4 When working the wrapped st, insert RH needle under the wrap and work it tog with the corresponding st on needle. next st on LH needle foll pat st.

SOCKS
BOTH BOYS' AND GIRLS' SOCKS
With A, cast 26 sts onto each needle—52 sts. Place marker for beg of rnd, join for knitting in the round. Work in k2, p2 ribbing for 16 rnds, change to B and work in St st and stripe pat as foll:
For girls' socks only
4 rnds B, 4 rnds A, 4 rnds B, 4 rnds C, 4 rnds A, 4 rnds B, 4 rnds A, 4 rnds B, 4 rnds C, 4 rnds A, 4 rnds B.
For boys' socks only
7 rnds B, 3 rnds C, 7 rnds B, 7 rnds A, 7 rnds B, 3 rnds C, 7 rnds B.

GIRL'S SOCKS
Turn heel
Change to A for short row heel as foll: Knit 13 sts and turn.
Next row Sl 1, p 12 sts from Needle 1, p 13 sts from Needle 2. Rearrange other sts to have 26 on each side, with the rnd beg in the middle of the heel.
Next row K25, w&t.
Next row P25, w&t.
Next row K to one st before wrapped st, w&t.
Next row P to one st before wrapped st, w&t.
Continue in this manner until you have 9 sts on each side wrapped and ready to start a knit row.
Knit to the first wrapped st on RS (not the first st you wrapped, but the first you

encounter on the needles when knitting), insert right-hand needle through the wrap and the st, knit them tog. Wrap next st on needle so there are two wraps around the st, turn.

Purl to first wrapped st on WS. With right-hand needle, lift the wrap and place on left-hand needle, purl this and the st tog. Wrap next st, turn.

To "unwrap" on RS rows, you will insert you right-hand needle through BOTH wraps AND the st, and knit all three tog. To "unwrap" on WS rows, simply lift up the wraps and place on the LH needle and purl together with the stitch. After you've unwrapped all stitches, you'll be ready to knit a RS row. With A, knit 13 sts on Needle 1 (to marker). Change to C and knit to end of needle.

Pick up 4 sts between Needles 1 and 2 in order to close any gaps caused by knitting the heel.

Knit sts on Needle 2. Switch to Needle 1 and pick up 4 sts between Needles 1 and 2 in order to close gaps.

Foot
Next rnd Knit to last 3 sts on Needle, k2tog, k1, knit sts onNeedle 2; needle 1 k1, ssk, k to end of rnd.

Next rnd Knit even.

Rep last 2 rows until you have a total of 26 sts on both needles, AND AT THE SAME TIME, continue with striping pat as foll:

4 rnds C, 4 rnds B, 4 rnds A, 4 rnds B, 4 rnds A, 4 rnds C, 4 rnds B.

Begin toe
On the last rnd of the third B stripe, dec 4 sts as foll: K to last 3 sts on Needle 1, k2tog, k1; Needle 2 k1, ssk, k to last 3 sts, k2tog, k1; Needle 1 k1, ssk, k to end of rnd—48 sts.

K 4 rnds in A.

Following the set stripe pattern of four rows per color in the CBABA sequence, work dec as foll:

Rnd 1 With B, *k4, k2tog; rep from * around—40 sts.

Rnd 2–7 Knit, switching to A on row 5.

Rnd 8 *K3, k3tog; rep from * around—32 sts.

Rnds 9–13 Knit, switching to C for rows 9-12 and then B for rnd 13.

Rnd 14 *K2, k2tog; rep from * around—24 sts.

Rnds 15–18 Knit, switching to A on rnd 17. Continue in A for rest of work.

Rnd 19 *K1, k2tog; rep from * around—16 sts.

Rnds 20–22 Knit.

Rnd 23 *K2tog; rep from * around—8 sts.

Cut long tail, thread through rem sts and cinch to close.

BOY'S SOCKS
Heel flap
Switch to A, dividing sts for heel flap as foll: k13 sts on Needle 1, turn. Purl 26 sts onto Needle 1 and redistribute rest of sts on Needle 2 so that both needles have 26 sts. Mark beg of rnd in the middle of Needle 1, this will come in handy when dec for gusset.

Heel flap is worked back and forth on Needle 1 as foll:
Row 1 *Sl 1, k1; rep from * to end.
Row 2 Sl 1, purl to end.
Rep rows 1 and 2 thirteen times or until flap measures approx 1¾"/4.5cm, ending with a row 2.

Turn heel
Row 1 Sl 1, k15, ssk, k1, turn.
Row 2 Sl 1, p7, p2tog, p1, turn.
Row 3 Sl 1, k8, ssk, k1, turn.
Row 4 Sl 1, p9, p2tog, p1, turn.
Cont working one more st than in previous row prior to the decrease, until you have 16 sts on Needle 1.

Gusset
Knit 8 sts in A, switch to C and finish sts on Needle 1. Pick up and knit 16 sts along flap edge, knit sts on needle 2. With Needle 1, pick up 16 sts on other side of flap, knit 8 sts to end of rnd—
Needle 1 40 sts, **Needle 2** 26 sts. Work gusset dec as foll:
Next (dec) rnd Needle 1 k to last 3 sts, k2tog, k1; **Needle 2** knit; **Needle 1** k1,

ssk, knit to marker.
Work dec rnd every other rnd until you have 26 sts on Needle 1, AT THE SAME TIME, work stripe pat as foll:
3 rnds C (first row is picking up sts row), 7 rnds B, 7 rnds A, 7 rnds B, 3 rnds C, 7 rnds B, 3 rnds C.

Begin toe
On the last rnd of the 2nd C stripe, work dec rnd as foll:
Needle 1 K10, k2tog, k1; **Needle 2** k1, ssk, k20, k2tog, k1; **Needle 1** k1, ssk, k to marker—48 sts.
Change to B and knit 2 rnds.
Rnd 1 *K4, k2tog; rep from * around—40 sts.
Rnds 2-6 Knit, switching at rnd 6 and continuing to end with A.
Rnd 7 *K3, k2tog; rep from * around—32 sts.
Rnds 8–11 Knit.
Rnd 12 *K2, k2tog; rep from * around—24 sts.
Rnds 13–15 Knit.
Rnd 16 *K1, k2tog; rep from * around—16 sts.
Rnds 17–18 Knit.
Rnd 19 *K2tog; rep from * around—8 sts.
Cut long tail, thread through rem sts and cinch to close.

FAUX-CABLE socks

David Lazurus

You'll Need

YARN ❶
- 1¾oz/50g, 230yd/210m of any fingering weight superwash wool and nylon blend yarn

NEEDLES
- One set (5) size 1 (2.25mm) double-pointed needles (dpns) *or size to obtain gauge*

OTHER MATERIALS
- Stitch marker

MEASUREMENTS
Foot circumference 8"/20.5cm
Length (heel to toe) 9½"/24cm

GAUGE
34 sts and 42 rnds to 4"/10cm over St st using size 1 (2.25mm) needles.
Take time to check your gauge.

STITCH GLOSSARY
Faux cable pattern
(over a multiple of 4 sts)
Rows 1, 2 and 3 *K2, p2; rep from * around.
Row 4 *K2tog without dropping from LH needle, insert RH needle between the 2 sts just knitted tog and k the first stitch again, slipping both sts from needle tog, p2*, rep from * around.
Rep rnds 1–4 for faux cable pattern.

SOCKS
With larger dpns, cast on 68 sts. Place marker and join, being careful not to twist sts. Work in cable pat until sock measures 6"/15cm from beg, end with a row 4.

TURN HEEL
Note Heel is worked back and forth on the first and last 17 sts of the rnd. This will put the beg of rnd in the center back of the sock.
Next rnd Work first 17 sts in pat, leaving next 34 sts on hold for instep, turn.
Next short row (WS) Sl 1, p33, removing marker for beg of rnd if necessary, turn.
Next short row Sl 1, k32, turn.
Cont in this way, always slipping first st and working 1 less st each row until there are 10 center sts with 12 slipped sts each side, ending with a k row. Do not turn. Insert RH needle under the strand between the last st worked and the next st (as for a M1) and k it tog with the next (slipped) st, turn.
Next row P11, insert point of RH needle under the last st worked and the next st (as for a M1) and p it tog with the next st, turn.
Cont in this way until all 34 heel sts have been worked, ending with a p (WS) row, turn. K17 sts onto one needle.
Next rnd With free needle, k17, pick up and k 4 sts along heel on same needle (Needle 1), work instep sts on Needles 2 and 3. With free needle (Needle 4) pick up and k 4 sts along heel, k17—76 sts.
Next rnd Work even.
Next (dec) rnd K to last 3 sts of Needle 1, k2tog, k1, work across instep sts to Needle 4, k1, SKP, k to end of rnd. Rep last 2 rnds 3 times more—68 sts. Work even until sock measures 8¼"/21cm or 1¾"/4.5cm less than desired length of foot.

SHAPE TOE
Next (dec) rnd K to last 3 sts of Needle 1, k2tog, k1; next needle k1, SKP, k to last 3 instep sts (on Needle 3), k2tog, k1; Needle 4 k1, SKP, k to end of rnd. K 1 rnd. Rep last 2 rnds 7 times more—36 sts. Then rep dec rnd every rnd 5 times more—16 sts. Arrange sts so there are 8 sts on each of 2 needles and graft closed.

David Lazurus

LACE CUFF
socks

David Lazurus

You'll Need

YARN
- 3½oz/100g, 460yd/420m of any fingering weight superwash wool and nylon blend yarn

NEEDLES
- One set (5) size 1 (2.25mm) double-pointed needles (dpns) *or size to obtain gauge*

OTHER MATERIALS
- Stitch marker

MEASUREMENTS
Foot circumference 8"/20.5cm
Length (heel to toe) 10"/25.5cm

GAUGE
34 sts and 42 rnds to 4"/10cm over St st using size 1 (2.25mm) dpns.
Take time to check your gauge.

STITCH GLOSSARY
LACE RIB PATTERN
(over a multiple of 7 sts)
Rnds 1–3 *K5, p2, rep from * around
Rnd 4 *K2tog, yo, k1, yo, ssk, p2; rep from * around.
Rep rnds 1-4 for lace rib pattern.

SOCKS
With size 1 (2.25mm) dpns, cast on 70 sts. Pm and join, being careful not to twist sts. Work in lace rib pat until sock measures 2"/5cm from beg.
Next rnd Work rnd 1 of lace pat dec 2 sts evenly around—68 sts. Change to St st (k every rnd) until sock measures 6"/15cm from beg.

TURN HEEL
Note Heel is worked back and forth on the first and last 17 sts of the rnd. This will put the beg of rnd in the center back of the sock.
Next rnd Work first 17 sts in pat, leaving next 34 sts on hold for instep, turn,
Next short row (WS) Sl 1, p33, removing marker for beg of rnd if necessary, turn.
Next short row Sl 1, k32, turn.
Cont in this way, always slipping first st and working 1 less st each row until there are 10 center sts with 12 slipped

sts each side, ending with a k row. Do not turn.
Insert RH needle under the strand between the last st worked and the next st (as for a M1) and k it tog with the next (slipped) st, turn.
Next row P11, insert point of RH needle under the last st worked and the next st (as for a M1) and p it tog with the next st, turn.
Cont in this way until all 34 heel sts have been worked, ending with a p (WS) row, turn. K17 sts onto one needle.
Next rnd With free needle, k17, pick up and k 4 sts along heel on same needle (Needle 1), work instep sts on Needles 2 and 3. With free needle (Needle 4) pick up and k 4 sts along heel, k17—76 sts.
Next rnd Work even.
Next (dec) rnd K to last 3 sts of Needle 1, k2tog, k1, work across instep sts to Needle 4, k1, SKP, k to end of rnd.
Rep last 2 rnds 3 times more—68 sts. Work even until sock measures 8¼"/21cm or 1¾"/4.5cm less than desired length of foot.

SHAPE TOE
Next (dec) rnd K to last 3 sts of Needle 1, k2tog, k1; next needle k1, SKP, k to last 3 instep sts (on Needle 3), k2tog, k1; Needle 4 k1, SKP, k to end of rnd. K 1 rnd. Rep last 2 rnds 7 times more—36 sts. Then rep dec rnd every rnd 5 times more—16 sts. Arrange sts so there are 8 sts on each of 2 needles and graft closed.

RIBBED socks

You'll Need

YARN
- 3½oz/100g, 330yd/300m of any self striping fingering weight wool yarn

NEEDLES
- One set (5) size 2 (2.75mm) double-pointed needles (dpns) *or size to obtain gauge*

OTHER MATERIALS
- Stitch marker

MEASUREMENTS
Foot circumference 8"/20.5cm
Length (heel to toe) 10"/25.5cm

GAUGE
25 sts and 36 rnds to 4"/10cm over St st using size 2 (2.75mm) needles. *Take time to check your gauge.*

STITCH GLOSSARY

M1 p-st With the needle tip, lift the strand between the last stitch worked and the next stitch on the left-hand needle and purl into back of it. One purl stitch has been added.

K2, P1 RIB (multiple of 3 sts)
Rnd 1 *K2, p1; rep from * around
Rep rnd 1 for rib pattern.

SOCKS

With size 2 (2.75mm) dpns, cast on 54 sts. Pm and join, being careful not to twist sts. Work in k2, p1 until sock measures 6"/15cm from beg.

TURN HEEL

Note Heel is worked on the first and last 14 sts of the rnd. This will put the beg of rnd in the center back of the sock.

David Lazarus

Next rnd K7, M1, k6 leaving next 28 sts on hold for instep, turn.
Next short row (WS) Sl 1, p20, M1 p-st, p6, removing marker for beg of rnd if necessary, turn.
Next short row Sl 1, k26, turn.
Next short row Sl 1, p25, turn. Cont in this way, always slipping first st and working 1 less st each row until there are 6 center sts with 11 slipped sts each side, ending with a k row. Do not turn. Insert point of RH needle under the last st worked and the next st (as for a M1) and k it tog with the next (slipped) st, turn.
Next row P7, insert point of RH needle under the last st worked and the next st (as for a M1) and p it tog with the next st, turn.
Cont in this way until all 28 heel sts have been worked, ending with a p (WS) row, turn. K14 sts onto one needle. Replace marker for beg of rnd. The beg of rnd is still in the same place.
Next rnd With free needle, k14, pick up and k 4 sts along heel on same needle (Needle 1), work instep sts in rib. With free needle (Needle 4) pick up and k 4 sts along heel, k14—64 sts.
Next rnd Cont in St st for sole of foot and

work in rib across instep sts.
Next (dec) rnd Work to last 3 sts of Needle 1, k2tog, k1, work across instep sts to Needle 4, k1, SKP, work to end of rnd.
Rep last 2 rnds 4 times more—54 sts. Work even until sock measures 8¼"/21cm or 1¾"/4.5cm less than desired length of foot.

SHAPE TOE

Next (dec) rnd K to last 3 sts of Needle 1, k2tog, k1; next needle k1, SKP, k to last 3 instep sts (on Needle 3), k2tog, k1; Needle 4 k1, SKP, k to end of rnd. K 1 rnd. Rep last 2 rnds 6 times more—26 sts. Then rep dec rnd every rnd 3 times more—14 sts. Arrange sts so there are 7 sts on each of 2 needles and graft closed.

FLIP FLOP socks

Rose Callahan

SIZE
To fit a women's shoe size 7½–8½ (women's 9½–men's 8½, men's 10½-12).

GAUGE
17 sts and 30 rows to 4"/10 cm over St st using size 8 (5 mm) needles. *Take time to check your gauge.*

SPECIAL TECHNIQUE
3-NEEDLE BIND-OFF
1 Hold right sides of pieces together on two needles. Insert third needle knitwise into first st of each needle, and wrap yarn knitwise
2 Knit these two sts together, and slep them off the needles. *Knit the next two sts together in the same manner.
3 Slip first st on 3rd needle over 2nd st and off needle. Rep from * in step 2 across row until all sts are bound off.

SOCKS
CUFF
With Winter White, cast on 36 (40, 44) sts and divide evenly over 4 needles. Join to work in rnds, being careful not to twist sts and place marker to mark beg of rnd.

Next rnd *K2, p2; rep from * to around. Work 5 more rnds in rib. Work even in St st until piece measures 5½ (6, 6½)"/14 (15, 16.5) cm from beg, or desired length to ankle. **Next rnd** Work heel sts with waste yarn as follows: with contrasting color waste yarn, k18 (20, 22), drop the waste yarn, slide sts to beginning of needle where you started, and knit these sts again with Sage.

Note From this point, work back and forth in rows, working each color section separately: winter white on top of foot; sage on sole. Work even until both pieces measure 6½ (6¾, 7)"/16.5 (17, 17.5) cm from waste yarn.

TOE
Working 18 (20, 22) sts with Sage, work as foll: **Dec rnd (RS)** Ssk, k to last 2 sts, k2tog. Work 1 rnd even. Rep last 2 rnds 3 (4, 5) times more—10 sts. Work Winter White sts in same way—10 sts on each of 2 needles. Use 3-Needle Bind-Off to join sts together.

HEEL
Carefully remove waste yarn and place sts from top and bottom heel opening on 2 needles—36 (40, 44) sts. Using Sage only, join yarn to one corner, picking up 1 extra st in each corner to close gaps—38 (42, 46) sts. Rearrange sts on four needles as follows: 9 (10, 11) sts on first and 3rd needles and 10 (11, 12) sts on 2nd and 4th needles. **Dec rnd** On first needle, SSK, work to end; on 2nd needle, k to last 2 sts, k2tog; on 3rd needle, SSK,

You'll Need
YARN ④
Lion Wool by Lion Brand Yarn Co. 3oz/85g, 158yd/144m (wool)
· 2 balls in #99 winter white, 1 ball in #123 sage

NEEDLES
· One set (5) size 8 (5mm) double-pointed needles (dpns) *or size to obtain gauge*

OTHER MATERIALS
· Yarn needle

work to end; on 4th needle, knit to last 2 sts, k2tog. Work 1 rnd even. Rep last 2 rnds 3 (4, 5) times more—22 sts. Sl sts from 2nd needle onto first needle; and sl sts from 4th needle onto 3rd needle—11 sts on each of 2 needles. Use 3-Needle Bind-Off to join the sts tog. Make 2nd sock as for first.

FINISHING
With Sage, embroider flip flop straps, being sure to make one for right and left. Sew top an bottom of foot together.

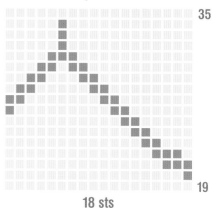

right foot

35

18 sts

19

color key
⬜ winter white
⬛ sage

HAPPY feet

You'll Need

YARN 4
- 3½oz/100g, 150yd/140m of any worsted weight cotton yarn

NEEDLES
- One pair size 8 (5mm) needles, *or size to obtain gauge*
- One set (4) size 8 (5mm) double-pointed needles (dpns)

OTHER MATERIALS
- Stitch markers and holders
- Two ⅞"/22mm buttons

MEASUREMENTS
Ankle circumference 8"/20.5cm
Foot Length 9"/23cm

GAUGE
18 sts and 24 rows to 4"/10cm over St st using size 8 (5mm) needles.
Take time to check your gauge.

STITCH GLOSSARY
Seed stitch (over an odd number of sts)
Every row *K1, p1; rep from * across row.

SOCKS
CUFF
Right sock
Cast on 49 sts. Work 4 rows in seed st.
Next (buttonhole) row (RS) Work 4 sts, bind-off 3, work to end.
Next row (WS) Work to bound off sts, cast on 3, work to end.
Work 4 more rows in seed st.
Next row Bind-off 13 sts in pat, work to end.
Place rem 36 sts on holder.

Left sock
Cast on 49 sts. Work 4 rows in seed st.
Next (buttonhole) row (RS) Work 42 sts, bind-off 3, work to end.
Next row (WS) Work to bound off sts, cast on 3 work to end.
Work 4 more rows in seed st.
Next row Work 36 sts, bind-off rem 13 sts in pat. Place 36 sts on holder.

HEEL
Note From here each sock is worked the same, one at a time. Transfer sts of one sock to dpns and arrange sts as foll: **Needle 1** 9 sts, **Needle 2** 18 sts, **Needle 3** 9 sts. Place marker and join for knitting in the round, taking care not to twist sts. Work 4 rnds in St st (knit every rnd).
Knit across Needle 1, work 18 sts on Needle #2 only for heel as foll:
Row 1 *Sl 1, k1; rep from * across 18 heel sts. Turn.
Row 2 Sl 1, p across. Turn.
Rep rows 1 and 2 nine times more.
Next row Sl 1, k11, SKP, turn.
Row 1 Sl 1, p5, p2tog, turn.
Row 2 Sl 1, k5, SKP, turn.
Rep last 2 rows until all sts have been worked, ending with a WS row—8 sts. K across all heel sts.

GUSSET
With free needle, pick up and knit 10 sts along edge of heel, plus one in corner. Knit across Needles 1 & 2, dropping marker when you come to it. Pick up and knit 10 sts along opposite edge of heel—48 sts. K to center of heel, place marker

Rose Callahan

for new beginning of round.
Redistribute sts as foll: **Needle 1** 15 sts, **Needle 2** 18 sts, **Needle 3** 15 sts.
Next (dec) rnd Needle 1 K to 3 sts from end, k2tog, k1; **Needle 2** knit; **Needle 3** k1, ssk, k to end. K 1 rnd even. Rep last 2 rnds until 36 sts rem.

INSTEP
Work even in St st until sock measures 7"/18cm from back of heel.

TOE
Next (dec) rnd Needle 1 K to last 3 sts from end, k2tog, k1;
Needle 2 k1, ssk, k to last 3 sts, k2tog, k1;
Needle 3 k1, ssk, k to end. K 1 rnd even. Rep last 2 rnds 3 times more—20 sts.
Work dec rnd each rnd 3 times more—8 sts.
Bind-off using 3-Needle Bind-Off (see page 8 for details).

FINISHING
Sew button to cuff opposite buttonhole.

PENGUIN SLIPPER
socks

Eye[4]Media, Bob Connors

You'll Need

YARN ③

- 3½oz/100g, 265yd/240m of any DK weight superwash merino wool yarn in grey (A)
- 1¾oz/50g, 135yd/120m in black (B) and a small amount in ecru for face (C)

NEEDLES

- One set (4) size 5 (3.75mm) double pointed needles (dpns) *or size to obtain gauge*

OTHER MATERIALS

- Stitch holder

KNITTED MEASUREMENTS

Leg width 4½ (6)"/11.5 (15)cm
Foot length 5½ (7½)"/14 (19)cm

GAUGE

20 sts and 28 rows/rnds to 4"/10cm over reverse St st using double strand of yarn and size 5 (3.75mm) dpns.
Take time to check your gauge.

SPECIAL TECHNIQUE

SHORT ROW WRAP & TURN (w&t)
(see page 2 for details)

NOTE

Work with double strand of yarn except for wings, beak and duplicate st embroidery. Slipper is knit with A on wrong side (k side), then is turned to right side (p side) after sock is finished.

SOCKS

CUFF

With double strand of A using one needle, loosely cast on 28 (36) sts. Divide sts on 3 needles with 9 (12) sts on Needle 1, 9 (12) sts on Needle 2 and 10 (12) sts on Needle 3. Join, taking care not to twist sts on needles. Mark end of rnd and sl marker every rnd. Work in k1, p1 rib for 2 (2½)"/5 (6.5)cm.

HEEL

Row 1 K 14 (18) sts and leave on needle for heel. Place rem 14 (18) sts on a st holder for instep.
Row 2 P13 (17), w&t.
Row 3 K12 (16), w&t
Row 4 P11 (15), w&t.
Row 5 K 10 (14), w&t.
Cont to work in this way having 1 less st each row until there are 4 (8) sts on last RS row.

Turn heel

Next row P5 (9), w&t.
Next row K6 (10), w&t. Then cont as foll:
Row 1 P6 (10), k1, w&t.
Row 2 P1, k6 (10), p1, w&t
Row 3 K1, p6 (10), k1, p1, w&t.
Row 4 K1, p1, k6 (10), p1, k1, w&t.
Row 5 P1, k1, p6 (10), k1, p2, w&t.
Row 6 K2, p1, k6 (10), p1, k2, w&t.
Row 7 P2, k1, p6 (10), k1, p3, turn.
Row 8 K3, p1, k6 (10), p1, k3.

FOOT

Rejoin to work in rnds, pm at beg of rnd as foll:
Next rnd Needle 1 K7 (9) sts from instep; **Needle 2** k7 (9) sts rem from instep; **Needle 3** work 14 (18) sts from heel, k the knit and p the purl sts. Cont working as established until foot measures 3 (4½)"/7.5 (11.5)cm from back of heel or 2½ (3)"/6.5 (7.5)cm less than total length of foot.

HEAD

Change to 2 strands B to complete foot.
Rnd 1 P18 (22), k6 (10), p4.
Rnd 2 K3 (5), p8, k6 (8), p1, k6 (10), p1, k3.
Rnd 3 K2 (4), p10, k5 (7), p1, k6 (10), p1, k3.
Rnd 4 K1 (3), p12, k4 (6), p1, k6 (10), p1, k3.
Rnd 5 K0 (2), p14, k3 (5), p1, k6 (10), p1, k3.

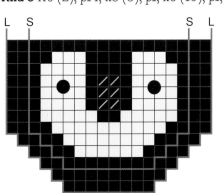

Color Key

■ Black (B)

□ Ecru (C) in duplicate st

● Black (B) in French knot

Rnd 6 K0 (1), p14 (16), k3 (4), p1, k6 (10), p1, k3.
Rep last rnd 6 (7) times more.

SHAPE TOE

Rnd 1 Needle 1 K1, p2tog, p to end; **Needle 2** p to last 3 sts, p2tog tbl, k1; **Needle 3** k1, k2tog tbl, p1, k to last 4 sts, p1, k2tog, k1.
Rnd 2 Needle 1 K1, p2tog, p to end; **Needle 2** p to last 3 sts, p2tog tbl, k1; **Needle 3** k1, k2tog tbl, k to last 3 sts, k2tog, k1.
Rep rnd 2 until there are 12 sts.
Next rnd [K2tog] 6 times. Cut yarn and pull through rem 6 sts and draw up tightly and secure end. Turn sock to RS (purl side of fabric).

WINGS

(make 2 for each slipper)
With single strand A, cast on 14 (16) sts on one needle. Divide sts on 3 needles with 4 (6) sts on Needle 1 and 5 sts on Needle 2 and 3. Join, taking care not to twist sts on needle. Mark end of rnd and sl marker every rnd. K 3 (4) rnds.
Next (inc) rnd K1, M1, k to last st, M1, k1. [Work 1 rnd even. Rep inc rnd] 1 (2) times—18 (22) sts. K 3 (4) rnds.
Rnd 1 K1, ssk, k to last 3 sts, k2tog, k1.
Rnd 2 Knit. Rep these 2 rnds 4 (6) times more—8 sts rem.
Next rnd [Ssk] twice, [k2tog] twice. Cut yarn and pull through rem 4 sts and draw up tightly and secure end.

FINISHING

Block socks being careful not to flatten rib. Block wings flat. Sew wings to head and tack tip of wings at rib foll photo.

FACE

With single strand of C, embroider face in duplicate st embroidery foll chart for chosen size. With double strand B, make 2 French knots for eyes and place as indicated by the black circles on chart.

BEAK

With double strand of B, pick up and k 6 sts at center of face as indicated by (/) on chart. Divide sts on 3 needles and join. K 2 rnds.
Next rnd [K2tog] 3 times. Cut yarn and pull through rem 3 sts and draw up tightly and secure end.

DOMINO SQUARE socks

Eye[4]Media, Bob Connors

You'll Need

YARN ①
- 3½oz/100g, 450yd/415m) of any fingering weight wool and nylon blend yarn in navy (A)
- 1¾oz/50g, 215yd/200m in rainbow multi (B)

NEEDLES
- One set (5) size 0 (2mm) double-pointed needles (dpns) *or size to obtain gauge*
- 1 larger size needle, for binding off

OTHER MATERIALS
- Stitch markers

KNITTED MEASUREMENTS
Leg width 7¼ (7½, 8, 8½)"/18.5 (19, 20.5, 21.5)cm
Foot length 8½ (9, 9½, 10)"/21 (22.5, 24, 25.5)cm

GAUGE
36 sts and 48 rows/rnds to 4"/10cm over St st using size 0 (2mm) dpn.
Take time to check gauge.

STITCH GLOSSARY
EYE OF PARTRIDGE ST
(even number of sts)
Row 1 *Sl 1, k1; rep from * to end.
Rows 2 and 4 Sl 1, purl to end.
Row 3 Sl 1, *sl 1, k1; rep from *, end k1.
Rep these 4 rows for eye of partridge st.

SPECIAL TECHNIQUE
SHORT ROW WRAP & TURN (w&t)
(see page 2 for details).

NOTE
To work RS join, on a RS row, sl the last st knitwise wyif, with the LH needle, pick up the 2 lps of the edge st on the adjoining strip, sl the last st back to LH needle and p this st and the lps tog. Turn, sl the first st knitwise wyib and purl across row. To work WS join, on a WS row, sl the last st knitwise wyib; with the LH needle, pick up the 2 lps of the edge st on the adjoining strip and k it; pass the sl st over. Turn, sl the first st purlwise and knit across row.

LARGE MITERED SQUARE—Chart 1
This square is placed on the top of the foot. Work back and forth in rows as foll: With A, cast on 65 (69, 73, 77) sts, pm at center st (use removable marker). **Row 1 (RS)** With A, knit. **Row 2** With A, k to center st, p1, k to end. Join B. **Row 3** With B, k to 1 st before center st, sl 2 sts as for k2tog without knitting them, k1, pass, the 2 sl sts over the k st (s2kp), k to end. **Row 4** With B, purl. Rep these 4 rows foll chart until 1 st rem. Cut color B, leaving this st on needle, with color A and RS facing, pick up and k 31 (33, 35, 37) sts across the top of the mitered square for 32 (34, 36, 38) sts.

TOE
With A, work in St st on these sts for 7 (7, 7, 9) rows.

Toe shaping
Row 1 Knit. **Row 2** Sl 1, p to last st, w&t. **Row 3** Sl 1, k to last st, w&t. **Row 4** Sl 1, p to 1 st before wrapped st, w&t. **Row 5** Sl 1, k to 1 st before wrapped st, w&t. Rep rows 4 and 5 until there are 16 (16, 18, 18) sts at center with 8 (9, 9, 10) sts wrapped on each side of toe. Then, cont to work underside of toe as foll: **Next row** Sl 1, p to wrapped st, pick up with wrap and p2tog, turn. **Next row** Sl 1, k to wrapped st, pick up with wrap and k2tog tbl, turn. Rep these 2 rows until all wrapped sts are worked and there are 32 (34, 36, 38) sts on needle.

SOLE
Next row With A, p to last st, p last st tog with 1 st from side edge of mitered square. **Next row** With A, k to last st, k last st tog with 1 st from side of mitered square. Cont to work sole in this way until all sts are joined to mitered square.

HEEL FLAP
Cont on the 32 (34, 36, 38) heel sts with A only, work 31 (33, 35, 37) rows in eye of partridge st.

TURN HEEL
Cont in the eye of partridge pat while turning heel, work as foll:
Row 1 (RS) Sl 1, work 20 (21, 23, 24) sts in eye of partridge st, ssk, turn.
Row 2 Sl 1, work 10 (10, 12, 12), p2tog, turn. **Row 3** Sl 1, work 10 (10, 12, 12) sts

Chart 2

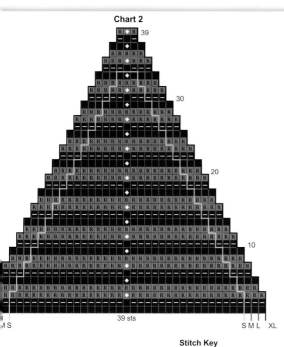

39

30

20

10

39 sts

M S

S M L XL

Needle 2 and 3 knit; **Needle 4** k1, ssk, k to end. **Rnd 2** Knit. Rep last 2 rnds until 64 (68, 72, 76) sts rem, end with rnd 2.

LEG
Note Leg will be composed of 8 small mitered squares, worked separately and joined while working.

With A, beg with the first st of the rnd, cast on 17 (18, 19, 20) sts at beg of rnd, then k these sts plus the 16 (17, 18, 19) sts on first needle for row 1 of mitered

square and a total of 33 (35, 37, 39) sts. Leave rem sts on rnd unworked. Place removable marker at center st. **Row 2 (WS)** With A, k to center st, p1, k to end. **Row 3** With B, k to 1 st before center st, s2kp, k to end. **Row 4** With B, purl. Work these 4 rows foll chart 2 until 1 st rem. Leaving this st on needle, with color A and RS facing, pick up and k 17 (18, 19, 20) sts down the side of the mitered square just worked, then k16 (17, 18, 19) sts from next instep sts of rnd—33 (35, 37, 39) sts for mitered square. Work as for previous small mitered square. Work 2 more mitered squares as before ONLY join the 4th mitered square to the end of the first mitered square using RS join. Then cont to work 4 more mitered squares across tops of these squares to complete cuff. Cut B.

TOP RIBBING
With last A lp on needle, pick up and k sts for a total of 64 (68, 72, 76) sts around or 16 (17, 18, 19) sts on each of 4 needles. Join and work in rnds of k2, p2 rib for 1½"/4cm. Bind-off loosely in rib.

FINISHING
Block socks, being careful not to flatten rib.

Chart 1

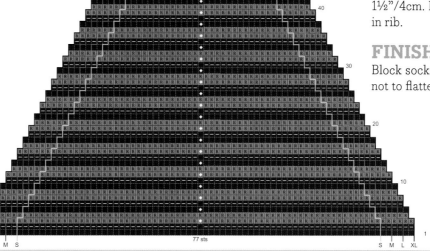

77

70

60

50

40

30

20

10

1

XL L M S

77 sts

S M L XL

Stitch Key

◼ K on RS, p on WS with Navy (A)

▭ P on RS, k on WS with Navy (A)

ℝ K on RS, p on WS with Rainbow (B)

◪ S2kp with Navy (A)

◩ S2kp with Rainbow (B)

in eye of partridge st, ssk, turn. Rep rows 2 and 3 until all sts are worked into heel turning—12 (12, 14, 14) sts. **Next rnd** With heel needle sts, pick up and k16 (17, 18, 19) sts along side (rows) of heel flap (Needle 1); pick up and k 32 (34, 36, 38) sts along side of mitered square and divide onto Needles 2 and 3, pick up and k 16 (17, 18, 19) sts along side (rows) of heel flap, k first half of heel sts with same needle (Needle 4)—a total of 76 (80, 86, 90) sts. Join and work in rnds. Pm at center back of heel to mark beg of rnd and sl marker every rnd.

SHAPE INSTEP
Rnd 1 Needle 1 K to last 3 sts, k2tog, k1;

Eye[4]Media, Bob Connors

LAVENDER LACE socks

KNITTED MEASUREMENTS
Leg width 7¼"/18.5cm
Foot length 8½"/21.5cm

GAUGE
40 sts and 54 rows/rnds to 4"/10cm over St st using size 0 (2mm) dpns.
Take time to check your gauge.

NOTE
Heel is knit with a reinforcing strand of yarn.

STITCH GLOSSARY
LACE PATTERN STITCH
(multiple of 9 sts)
Rnd 1 *P1, k7, p1; rep from * around.
Rnd 2 *P1, yo, k2, SK2P, k2, yo, p1; rep from * around.
Rnds 3 and 5 Rep rnd 1.
Rnd 4 *P1, k1, yo, k1, SK2P, k1, yo, k1, p1; rep from * around.
Rnd 6 *P1, k2, yo, SK2P, yo, k2, p1; rep from * around.
Rep rnds 1-6 for lace pat st.

SOCKS
CUFF
Using one needle, loosely cast on 72 sts. Divide sts on 4 needles with 18 sts on each needle. Join, taking care not to twist sts on needles. Mark end of rnd and sl marker every rnd. P 1 rnd. Beg with rnd 1, work in lace pat st, working 9-st rep 8 times around, until piece measures 7½"/19cm from beg, end with rnd 6,

stretching slightly (or trying on to fit).

HEEL
Turn work. Sl 1, p35 heel sts. Leave rem 36 sts on 2 needles to be worked later for instep.
Row 2 (RS) Add another strand of yarn (reinforcing yarn) and *sl 1, k1; rep from * to end.
Row 3 Sl 1, p35.
Rep rows 2 and 3 until heel measures 2¼"/6cm, end with a RS row.
Turn heel
Row 1 Sl 1, p20, p2tog, p1, turn.
Row 2 Sl 1, k7, ssk, k1, turn.
Row 3 Sl 1, p8, p2tog, p1, turn.
Row 4 Sl 1, k9, ssk, k1, turn.
Row 5 Sl 1, p10, p2tog, p1, turn.
Row 6 Sl 1, k11, ssk, k1, turn.
Row 7 Sl 1, p12, p2tog, p1, turn.
Row 8 Sl 1, k13, ssk, k1, turn.
Row 9 Sl 1, p14, p2tog, p1, turn.
Row 10 Sl 1, k15, ssk, k1, turn.
Row 11 Sl 1, p16, p2tog, p1, turn.
Row 12 Sl 1, k17, ssk, k1, turn.
Row 13 Sl 1, p18, p2tog, p1, turn.
Row 14 Sl 1, k19, ssk, k1—22 sts. Cut reinforcing yarn.
With first needle, pick up and k18 sts along side (rows) of heel (Needle 1); [p1, k7, p1] twice (Needle 2); [p1, k7, p1] twice (Needle 3); pick up and k18 sts along side (rows) of heel and k11 sts from Needle 1, sl rem 11 sts onto first needle—there are 29 sts on first and fourth needles and 18 sts on 2nd and 3rd needles and a total of 94 sts.

SHAPE INSTEP
Rnd 1 Needle 1 K11, [k1 tbl] 15 times, k2tog, k1 tbl; **Needles 2 and 3** work even in lace pat st; **Needle 4** k1 tbl, ssk, [k1tbl] 15 times, k11.
Rnd 2 Needle 1 Knit; **Needles 2 and 3** work even in lace pat st; **Needle 4** knit.

You'll Need
YARN ①
· 3½oz/100g, 415yd/380m of any fingering weight super-wash wool yarn

NEEDLES
· One set (5) size 0 (2mm) double-pointed needles (dpns) *or size to obtain gauge*

Rnd 3 Needle 1 K to last 3 sts, k2tog, k1; **Needles 2 and 3** work even in lace pat st; **Needle 4** k1, ssk, k to end.
Rnd 4 Rep rnd 2. Rep rnd 3 and 4 until 72 sts rem and there are 18 sts on each needle. Work even as established until foot measures 7"/18cm from back of heel or 1½"/4cm less then desired length of foot (try on sock to ensure the correct length).

SHAPE TOE
Rnd 1 Knit.
Rnd 2 Needle 1 K to last 3 sts, k2tog, k1; **Needle 2** k1, ssk, k to end; **Needle 3** k to last 3 sts, k2tog, k1; **Needle 4** k1, ssk, k to end.
Rnd 3 Knit.
Rep rnds 2 and 3 eight times more—36 sts rem. Then rep rnd 2 four times more—20 sts rem. Reposition sts as necessary on last rnd: **Needle 1** K3, k2tog, k1; **Needle 2** k1, ssk, k3 sts from **Needle 3**, k2tog, k1; **Needle 3** k1, ssk, k3, k4 from **Needle 1**—16 sts rem. Divide sts evenly onto 2 needles and weave toe sts tog using Kitchener st.

FINISHING
Block socks stretching slightly lengthwise.

RIB AND PANEL socks

Eye[4]Media, Bob Connors

You'll Need

YARN 1
- 3½ oz/100g, 350yd/320m of any fingering weight merino wool yarn in red (A)
- 1¾oz/50g, 175yd/165m in red multi (B)

NEEDLES
- One set (4) size 3 (3.25mm) double-pointed needles (dpns) *or size to obtain gauge*

KNITTED MEASUREMENTS
Leg width 7½"/19cm
Foot length 8"/20.5cm

GAUGE
29 sts and 35 rows/rnds to 4"/10cm over St st using size 3 (3mm) dpns.
Take time to check your gauge.

SOCKS
CUFF
Roll A into 2 balls. With A, cast on 20 sts, with B cast on 14 sts, with second ball of A cast on 20 sts—54 sts.
Row 1 (RS) With A [k3, p2] 4 times, with B k14, with A [p2, k3] 4 times.
Next row With A [p3, k2] 4 times, with B p14, with A [k2, p3] 4 times.
Repeat these 2 rows until 5"/12cm from beg, end with a WS row.

Separate for heel
Next row(RS) Sl first 13 sts to a holder for heel, work across in pat to last 13 sts for instep, sl these 13 sts to sep holder for heel.

INSTEP
Next row With A cont in rib over 7 sts, with B purl 14, with A cont in rib over 7 sts—28 sts.
Work back and forth in rows as established until instep measures 5.5"/14cm. Place 28 instep sts on holder.

HEEL
Return to 26 heel sts and work even in rows of rib for 20 rows.
Turn heel
Row 1 (RS) K18, SKP, turn.
Row 2 Sl 1, p10, p2tog, turn.
Row 3 Sl 1, k10, SKP, turn.
Row 4 Rep row 2.
Rep last 2 rows until 12 sts rem, end with

a p row. Cut yarn.

SHAPE INSTEP
With spare needle and A, pick up and k 14 sts along right side of heel, k6 sts of heel on same needle, with another needle, k rem 6 heel sts, pick up and k 14 sts along left side of heel—40 sts.
Next row Purl.
Next row K1, SKP, k to last 3 sts, k2tog, k1.
Next row K1, p to last st, k1.
Rep last 2 rows until there are 28 heel sts.

FOOT
Work even in St st on these sts until there are same number of rows as instep.
Shape toe
Reposition sts beg at last 14 sts of foot (Needle 1), 28 sts of instep (Needle 2), rem 14 sts of foot (Needle 3). Rejoin yarn to work in rnds for toe with A only.
Rnd 1 Knit.
Rnd 2 Needle 1 K to last 3 sts, k2tog, k1; **Needle 2** k1, SKP, k to last 3 sts, k2tog, k1; **Needle 3** k1, SKP, k to end. Rep these 2 rnds until 16 sts rem. Divide sts onto 2 needles and weave toe sts tog using Kitchener st.

FINISHING
Block socks, being careful not to flatten rib. Sew back leg, instep and foot seams.

TWO-NEEDLE
socks

Eye[4]Media, Bob Connors

KNITTED MEASUREMENTS
Leg width 7½"/19cm
Foot length 8 (9)"/20.5 (23)cm

GAUGE
28 sts and 28 rows to 4"/10cm over k1, p1 rib using larger needles.
Take time to check your gauge.

SOCKS
Beg at cuff edge with larger needles and A, cast on 25 sts.
Row 1 (RS) K1, [k1, p1] 11 times, k2.
Row 2 K1, [p1, k1] 12 times.
Rep these 2 rows for k1, p1 rib for 10 (12)"/25.5 (30.5)cm. This forms the leg and instep.

SHAPE TOE
Change to smaller needle. Place yarn markers for toe after the first st and before the last st, inserting scrap yarn from back to front between the sts on each end of row. Work even for 2½"/6.5cm.

SOLE
Change to larger needles. Place yarn markers for the sole after the first st and before the last st, inserting scrap yarn from front to back between the sts on each end of row (figure 1). Work even for 5 (6)"/12.5 (15cm) from last markers.

SHAPE HEEL
Change to smaller needles. Place yarn markers for the heel after the first st and before the last st, inserting scrap yarn from back to front between the

You'll Need
YARN ③
- 3½oz/100g balls 275yd/255m of any DK weight wool yarn in aqua (A)
- Small amounts in teal (B)

NEEDLES
- One pair each sizes 1 and 4 (2.25 and 3.5mm) needles *or size to obtain gauge*

OTHER MATERIALS
- Size E/4 (3.5mm) crochet hook
- Tapestry needle

sts on each end of row. Work even for 2½"/6.5cm from last markers.

BACK LEG
Change to larger needles. Place yarn marker for the back leg after the first st and before the last st, inserting scrap yarn from front to back between the sts on each end of row. Work even for 5 (6)"/12.5 (15)cm from last markers. Total length is 25 (29)"/63.5 (73.5)cm. Bind-off loosely in rib.

FINISHING
With WS tog, tie the two ends of each set of markers as shown (figure 2).

LEG SEAMS
Beg at the top of the leg seam with RS facing, stitch tog with B, making sure that the seam is loose enough to stretch with the rest of the knitting as foll: insert needle from the back to the front of the first garter-st ridge on the right piece, insert the needle from front to back on the first garter-st ridge on the left piece then from back to front on the 2nd ridge on right piece. Cont to work in this way inserting from front to back on the left

Figure 1

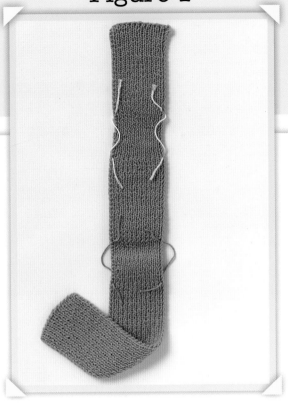

Figure 2

piece and back to front on the right piece up to the heel marker. Cont to stitch past the heel marker (leaving the sts tied off by the marker for heel seam—figure 3). Cont stitching to the toe marker, remove marker and cont stitching until the seam is completely closed. Leave a 10"/26cm tail on the outside.

Figure 3

HEEL SEAM
Remove heel marker. Beg at the left seam, work to the end of heel seam stitching as before. When closed, leave a 10"/26cm tail on the outside. Work other heel seam in same way.

REINFORCING HEEL AND TOE
Using the tail, weave across the toe seam 3 times. Reinforce heel in same way.

CROCHET EDGING
With crochet hook and B, sl st into first joining st at top of sock, *skip 1 purl st, ch 3, sl st into next k st; rep from * around, end with a sl st into first sl st. Fasten off. Wash and block socks flat to dry.

STRIPED PATCHWORK socks

Eye[4]Media, Bob Connors

You'll Need

YARN 4

- 1¾oz/50g, 225yd/205m of any worsted weight wool yarn each in forest green (MC), dark taupe (A), light taupe (B), olive (C), black (D), rust (E), burgundy (F) and gold (G)

NEEDLES

- One pair size 6 (4mm) needles *or size to obtain gauge*
- One set (4) size 6 (4mm) double-pointed needles (dpns)

OTHER MATERIALS

- Stitch holder

KNITTED MEASUREMENTS

Leg width 8¾"/22cm
Foot length 9½"/24cm

GAUGE

22 sts and 28 rows/rnds to 4"/10cm over St st using size 6 (4mm) needles.
Take time to check gauge.

NOTE

When changing colors, twist yarns on WS to prevent holes.

LEFT SOCK

CUFF

With MC and straight needles, cast on 48 sts. **Row 1 (RS)** *K2, p2; rep from * to end. Work in k2, p2 rib as established for 3½"/9cm.
Beg leg chart
Next row (RS) Knit, foll row 1 of chart. Cont in St st and color pat foll leg chart through row 50. Change to dpns.

HEEL

Sl last 12 sts of row onto one dpn, then first 12 sts of row onto same needle—24 heel sts. Sl rem 24 sts to a st holder for instep. **Row 1 (RS)** With MC, *sl 1, k1; rep from * to end.
Row 2 Sl 1, p to end. Rep last 2 rows until heel measures 2¼"/6cm, end with a RS row.
Turn heel
Row 1 (WS) P15, p2tog, p1, turn.
Row 2 Sl 1, k7, SKP, k1, turn.
Row 3 Sl 1, p8, p2tog, p1, turn.
Row 4 Sl 1, k9, SKP, k1, turn.
Row 5 Sl 1, p10, p2tog, p1, turn.
Row 6 Sl 1, k11, SKP, k1, turn.
Row 7 Sl 1, p12, p2tog, p1, turn.
Row 8 Sl 1, k13, SKP, k1—16 sts.
Cut MC.
Next rnd (RS) With MC, pick up and k 11 sts along left side (rows) of heel (Needle 1); k 24 sts of instep (Needle 2);

pick up and k 11 sts along right side of heel, k 8 sts from heel onto end of needle (Needle 3); sl rem 8 heel sts onto end of Needle 1—62 total sts.

SHAPE INSTEP

Rnd 1 Needle 1 k to last 3 sts, k2tog, k1; **Needle 2** knit; **Needle 3** k1, ssk, knit to end.
Rnd 2 With E, knit.
Rnd 3 With E, rep rnd 1.
Rnd 4 With MC, knit
Rnd 5 With MC, rep rnd 1.
Rnd 6 With E, knit.
Rnd 7 With E, rep rnd 1.
Rnd 8 With A, knit.
Rnd 9 With A, rep rnd 1.
Rnd 10 With C, knit.
Rnd 11 With C, rep rnd 1.
Rnd 12 With A, knit.
Rnd 13 With A, rep rnd 1—48 sts. Beg

with rnd 15, work in stripe pat foll foot chart and cont through rnd 50 of chart.

SHAPE TOE
Cont with MC only, work as foll:
Rnd 1 Needle 1 k to last 3 sts, k2tog, k1;
Needle 2 k1, ssk, k to last 3 sts, k2tog, k1;
Needle 3 k1, ssk, k to end of Needle 3.
Rnd 2 Knit. Rep last 2 rnds 5 times more—24 sts. Divide sts evenly onto 2 needles and weave toe sts tog using Kitchener st.

RIGHT SOCK
Work as for left sock, reversing placement of patchwork square on leg chart.

FINISHING
Block socks being careful not to flatten rib. Sew leg seam, sewing last half of rib from RS for cuff turnback.

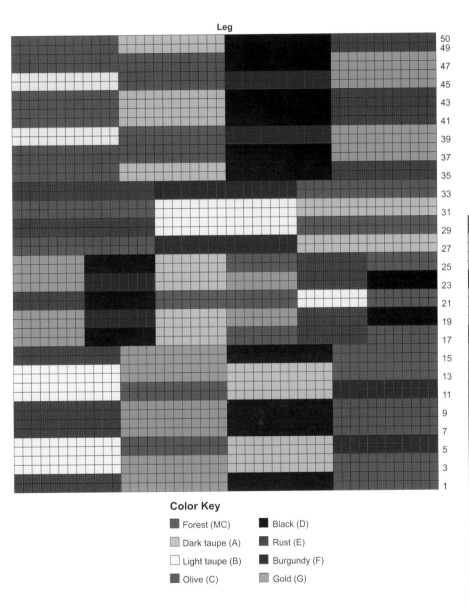

Leg

Foot

Color Key

- Forest (MC)
- Dark taupe (A)
- Light taupe (B)
- Olive (C)
- Black (D)
- Rust (E)
- Burgundy (F)
- Gold (G)

GIRL'S ANKLE socks

Eye[4]Media, Bob Connors

You'll Need

YARN

- 1¾oz/50g, 190yd/175m of any fingering weight merino wool yarn

NEEDLES

- 1 set (5) size 1 (2.25mm) double-pointed needles (dpns) *or size to obtain gauge*

OTHER MATERIALS

- Stitch holder

KNITTED MEASUREMENTS

Leg width 6"/15cm
Foot Length 6 (7)"/15 (18)cm

GAUGE

32 sts and 42 rows/rnds to 4"/10cm over St st using size 1 (2.25mm) dpns. *Take time to check your gauge.*

SOCKS

CUFF

Using one needle, cast on 56 sts. Divide sts on 4 needles with 14 sts on each needle. Join, taking care not to twist sts on needles. Mark end of rnd and sl marker every rnd.
Foundation rnd *K1, p1; rep from * around.
Beg lace pat
Rnd 1 *K1, yo, [p1, k1] twice, p1, SK2P, [p1, k1] twice, p1, yo; rep from * around.
Rnd 2 *K2, [p1, k1] 6 times; rep from * around.
Rnd 3 *K1, yo, [k1, p1] twice, k1, SK2P, [k1, p1] twice, k1, yo; rep from * around.
Rnd 4 *K1, p1; rep from * around. Work rnds 1–4 once more.
Next rnd [K5, k2tog] 8 times—48 sts. Cont in St st (k every rnd) until 2"/5cm are worked in St st.

HEEL

Next row With spare needle, k18, sl next 24 sts onto 2 needles for instep to be worked later. Turn and sl 1, p23—24 heel sts.
Row 1 *Sl 1, k1; rep from * to end.
Row 2 Sl 1, p23.
Rep these 2 rows 11 times more (25 rows in heel).

Turn heel

Row 1 Sl 1, k13, ssk, k1, turn.
Row 2 Sl 1, p5, p2tog, p1, turn.
Row 3 Sl 1, k6, ssk, k1, turn.
Row 4 Sl 1, p7, p2tog, p1, turn.
Cont to work in this way until there are 14 sts in heel, ending with a purl row (the last 2 rows will have the last 2 sts of row dec'd).

SHAPE INSTEP

Next rnd Needle 1 K14 heel sts, pick up and k12 sts along side (rows) of heel (Needle 1); **Needle 2** k24 sts of instep; **Needle 3** pick up and k 12 sts along side (rows) of heel, k7 sts from Needle 1—62 sts.
Rnd 1 Needle 1 K to last 3 sts, k2tog, k1; **Needle 2** knit; **Needle 3** k1, ssk, k to end.
Rnd 2 Knit.
Rep these 2 rnds 6 times more—48 sts rem. Cont in St st until foot measures 4½ (5½)"/11 (14)cm from back of heel or 1½"/4cm less than desired length of foot.

SHAPE TOE

Rnd 1 Needle 1 K to last 3 sts, k2tog, k1; **Needle 2** k1, ssk, k to last 3 sts, k2tog, k1; **Needle 3** k1, ssk, k to end.
Rnd 2 Knit. Rep last 2 rows 6 times more—20 sts rem.
Then rep rnd 1 three times more—8 sts. Cut yarn leaving a 9"/23cm end. Draw yarn through rem sts and pull up tightly to secure.

FINISHING

Block socks being careful not to flatten.

TEXTURED socks

You'll Need

YARN (4)
- 5oz/150g, 250yd/230m of any worsted weight wool and alpaca blend yarn each in red multi and purple multi

NEEDLES
- 1 set (5) size 8 (5mm) double-pointed needles (dpns) *or size to obtain gauge*

OTHER MATERIALS
- Small amounts of waste yarn

Eye[4]Media, Bob Connors

KNITTED MEASUREMENTS
Leg width 8"/20.5cm
Foot length 9"/23cm

GAUGE
18 sts and 24 rows/rnds to 4"/10cm over St st using size 8 (5mm) needles.
Take time to check your gauge.

STITCH GLOSSARY
CUFF PATTERN STITCH
(multiple of 4 sts)
Note Pat st is worked in rnds.
Rnd 1 *P3tog leaving sts on LH needle, yo, p same 3 sts tog again and sl from needle, k1; rep from * around.
Rnd 2 Knit.
Rnd 3 *K1, p3tog leaving sts on LH needle, yo, p same 3 sts tog again and sl from needle; rep from * around.
Rnd 4 Knit.
Rep rnds 1-4 for cuff pat st.

SOCKS
CUFF
With one needle and A, cast on 48 sts. Divide sts evenly on 4 needles with 12 sts on each needle. Join, taking care not to twist sts on needles. Mark end of rnd and sl marker every rnd. Work in k2, p2 rib for 4 rnds. Then cont in cuff pat st, alternating 2 rnds A and 2 rnds B, until 24 rnds are worked in cuff pat st. Keep A & B yarns attached.
Next rnd With waste yarn, k next 24 sts. With B, k same 24 sts.
Next rnd With B, [k2, k2tog] 12 times around—9 sts rem on each of 4 needles and there are a total of 36 sts.
Work even in St st with B (k every rnd) until 5½"/14cm are worked even in St st. Change to A and k 4 rnds.

SHAPE TOE
Next rnd Needle 1 K1, ssk, k to end;
Needle 2 k to last 3 sts, k2tog, k1;
Needle 3 as for Needle 1; **Needle 4** as for Needle 2. Rep last rnd 4 times more—16 sts rem. Divide sts evenly onto 2 needles and weave toe sts tog using Kitchener st.

HEEL
Remove waste yarn (there are 24 A sts below the waste yarn and 24 B sts above the waste yarn), and carefully place the 48 sts on 4 needles with 12 sts on each needle. Pm at inside corner of heel to mark beg of rnd.
Next rnd With A, *k2, k2tog; rep from * around, picking up 1 st at each inside corner of heel—38 sts.
K 1 rnd. Next rnd Working into last st of previous rnd as first st, sl 2 sts knitwise, k1, psso, (S2KP), k to 1 st before next corner st, S2KP, k to end of rnd**.
Rep between **'s 4 times more—18 sts. Divide sts evenly onto 2 needles and weave sts tog using Kitchener st.

SECOND SOCK
Work as for first sock reversing colors A and B.

FINISHING
Block socks being careful not to flatten rib.

DIAMOND LACE socks

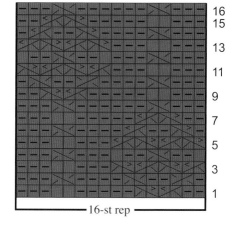

KNITTED MEASUREMENTS
Leg width 8¼"/21cm
Foot length 8½"/21.5cm

GAUGE
31 sts and 36 rnds to 4"/10cm over cable pat foll chart using size 3 (3mm) dpn.
Take time to check gauge.

STITCH GLOSSARY
1/1 RPC Sl 1 st to cn and hold to *back*, k1, then p1 from cn.
1/1 LPC Sl 1 st to cn and hold to *front*, p1, then k1 from cn.
C2R Sl 1 st to cn and hold to *back*, k1, then k1 from cn.
C2L Sl 1 st to cn and hold to *front*, k1, then k1 from cn.
SSP Sl 2 sts knitwise one at a time, return these 2 sts to LH needle and p2tog tbl.

Baby cable ribbing (multiple of 4 sts)
Rnd 1 *C2L, p2; rep from * around.
Rnd 2 *K2, p2; rep from * around.
Rep these 2 rnds for baby cable ribbing.

SOCKS
CUFF
Using one needle, cast on 64 sts. Divide sts on 4 needles with 16 sts on each needle. Join, taking care not to twist sts on needles. Mark end of rnd and sl marker every rnd. Work baby cable rib for 12 rnds, then work rnd 1 once more. On last rnd, remove rnd marker, sl 1 st and place new rnd marker (rnd is now positioned 1 st to the left to line up with the cable pat chart). Work rnd 1 of cable pat chart working 16-st rep 4 times and repositioning by one st on each needle, so that a complete rep is on each of the 4 needles. Cont to foll chart through rnd 16, then rep rnds 1–16 once, rnds 1–8 once.

HEEL
With spare needle, beg at right edge of heel, k2, p1, then sl the 27 sts from end of rnd to other end of same needle for heel, divide rem 34 sts onto 2 needles to be worked later for instep.
Next row (WS) Sl 1, k1, p26, k2.
Next row (RS) Sl 1, k29. Rep these 2 rows until there are 31 rows in heel.
Turn heel
Row 1 (RS) Sl 1, k14, ssk, k1, turn.
Row 2 Sl 1, p1, p2tog, p1, turn.
Row 3 Sl 1, k3, ssk, k1, turn.
Row 4 Sl 1, p5, p2tog, p1, turn.
Row 5 Sl 1, k7, ssk, k1, turn.
Row 6 Sl 1, p9, p2tog, p1, turn.
Row 7 Sl 1, k11, ssk, k1, turn.
Row 8 Sl 1, p13, p2tog, p1, turn.
Row 9 Sl 1, k15, ssk, k1, turn.
Row 10 Sl 1, p17, p2tog, p1, turn—20 sts.
With spare needle, k20, pick up and k 16 sts along side (rows) of heel, p1, (Needle 3), pm for beg of rnd, cont 32 sts in cable pat as established (Needle 1), p1, pick up and k 16 sts along side (rows) of heel—86 sts. K all sts around to 2 sts before beg of rnd.

SHAPE INSTEP
*Ssp, work 32 sts of Needle 1, p2tog, k until 2 sts before beg of rnd (2 sts dec'd). Rep from * 10 times more—64 sts. Reposition sts so that there are 16 sts on Needles 2 and 3 and 32 sts on Needle 1 and cont in pats as established until there are a total of five 16-rnd reps along instep from beg of sock. Work rnds 1–8 once, foot measures 6½"/16.5cm from back of heel.

SHAPE TOE
Rnd 1 Needle 1 K1, ssk, k to last 3 sts, k2tog, k1; **Needle 2** k1, ssk, k to end; **Needle 3** k to last 3 sts, k2tog, k1.
Rnd 2 Knit.
Rep last 2 rnds 8 times more—28 sts rem. Divide sts evenly onto 2 needles and weave toe sts tog using Kitchener st.

FINISHING
Block socks being careful not to flatten rib.

You'll Need
YARN ③
- 5¼oz/150g, 410yd/375m of any DK weight superwash wool yarn

NEEDLES
- 1 set (5) size 3 (3mm) double-pointed needles (dpns) *or size to obtain gauge*

OTHER MATERIALS
- Cable needle (cn)
- Stitch marker

CABLE PATTERN

16
15
13
11
9
7
5
3
1

— 16-st rep —

Stitch Key

☐ K on RS, p on WS

⊟ P on RS, k on WS

▱ 1/1 RPC

▱ 1/1 LPC

▱ C2R

▱ C2L

STRIPED SHEEP socks

KNITTED MEASUREMENTS

Leg width 8¾"/22cm
Foot length 10"/25.5cm

GAUGE

22 sts and 30 rows/rnds to 4"/10cm over St st using larger dpns.
Take time to check your gauge.

NOTE

Sheep are embroidered foll chart using duplicate st after the socks are knit.

SOCKS

CUFF

Using one smaller needle, with A, cast on 48 sts. Divide sts on 3 needles with 16 sts on each needle. Join, taking care not to twist sts on needles. Mark end of rnd and sl marker every rnd. Working in k2, p2 rib, work 1 rnd with A, 4 rnds with B, 3 rnds with A, 3 rnds with B.

Change to larger dpn. Then cont in St st (k every rnd) with B for 20 rnds.
Next rnd *K2 with D, k2 with A; rep from * around. Rep this rnd once more. Then work 2 rnds C, 2 rnds B, 2 rnds A and 2 rnds D.

HEEL

Sl last 12 sts from needle 3 onto spare needle, then sl first 12 sts from Needle 1 onto other end of same needle—24 heel sts. Divide rem 24 sts onto 2 needles to be worked later for instep. Work on 24 heel sts with B back and forth in rows.
Row 1 (WS) With B, sl 1, p to end.
Row 2 *Sl 1, k1; rep from * to end. Rep these 2 rows until there are 17 rows in heel.

TURN HEEL

Row 1 K14, ssk, k1, turn.
Row 2 Sl 1, p5, p2tog, p1, turn.
Row 3 Sl 1, k6, ssk, k1, turn.
Row 4 Sl 1, p7, p2tog, p1, turn.
Cont to work heel shaping in this way, working 1 more st between dec's each row until all sts are worked—14 sts.
Next rnd (RS) With A, sl first 7 sts onto spare needle. With another spare needle, k7 (the rem heel sts) then with same needle, pick up and k 12 sts along side (rows) of heel, (Needle 1), pm; with Needle 2, k24 sts of instep, pm; with Needle 3, pick up and k12 sts along side (rows) of heel, k7 rem heel sts—62 sts.

SHAPE INSTEP

Rnd 1 K to 2 sts before first marker, k2tog, k to 2nd marker, sl marker and ssk, k to end. K 1 rnd. Rep last 2 rnds 6 times more, AT THE SAME TIME, work stripes working a total of 4 rnds with A (including pick-up rnd), 2 rnds D, 3 rnds A, then cont with C for 6 rnds—48 sts after instep shaping is completed. Then cont stripe pat, with 4 rnds more with C, 2 rnds A, 14 rnds B, 2 rnds A, 3 rnds D, then cont with B for 8 rnds or until foot measures 8"/20.5cm from back of heel or 2"/5cm less than desired length of foot.

SHAPE TOE

Cont with A only and divide sts on 3 needles as foll: 12 sts on Needle 1, 24 sts on Needle 2, 12 sts on Needle 1.
Rnd 1 Needle 1 K to last 3 sts, k2tog, k1; Needle 2 k1, ssk, k to last 3 sts, k2tog, k1; Needle 3 k1, ssk, k to end.
Rnd 2 Knit. Rep last 2 rnds 5 times more—24 sts rem. Divide sts evenly onto 2 needles and weave toe sts tog using Kitchener st.

FINISHING

Centering sheep chart on one side of cuff section in A, embroider sheep foll chart using duplicate st. Work another sheep on opposite side of cuff. Work other sock in same way. Block socks being careful not to flatten rib.

Color Key

■ Black (B)
■ Grey (C)
☐ Cream (E)

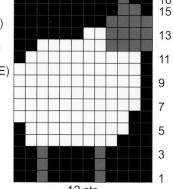

12 sts

Eye[4]Media, Bob Connors

TEXTURED
fair-isle socks

Eye[4]Media, Bob Connors

You'll Need

YARN ③
- 3½oz/100g balls, 260yd/240m of any DK weight machine washable merino yarn in navy (MC)
- 1¾oz/50g, 130yd/120m in dark green (A), light blue (B), denim blue (C), and light green (D)

NEEDLES
- One set (4) size 5 (3.75mm) double-pointed needles (dpns) or size to obtain gauge

OTHER MATERIALS
- Stitch holder

KNITTED MEASUREMENTS
Leg width 9½"/24cm
Foot length 10"/25.5cm

GAUGE
25 sts and 33 rows/rnds to 4"/10cm over St st foll chart using size 5 (3.75mm) needles.
Take time to check your gauge.

NOTE
When changing colors, twist yarns on WS to prevent holes. Purl sts on chart in background color are indicated with purl symbol (-).

CUFF
Beg at top edge, with MC cast on 60 sts. Divide sts on three needles with 20 sts on each needle. Join, taking care not to twist sts on needles. Mark end of rnd and sl marker every rnd. Work around in k1, p1 rib for 1½"/4cm. Then foll chart 1, work 10-st rep 6 times. Work through row 19 of chart 1. Then foll chart 2, work 6-st rep 10 times. Work through row 22 of chart 2.

HEEL
Sl last 15 sts of Needle 3 and first 15 sts of Needle 1 onto one dpn—30 heel sts. Sl rem 30 sts to a holder for instep.
Row 1 (RS) With MC, *sl 1, k1; rep from * to end.
Row 2 Sl 1, p to end.
Rep last 2 rows until heel measures 2¼"/6cm, end with a RS row.

Turn heel
Row 1 (WS) P17, p2tog, p1, turn.
Row 2 Sl 1, k5, SKP, k1, turn.
Row 3 Sl 1, p6, p2tog, p1, turn.
Row 4 Sl 1, k7, SKP, k1, turn.
Row 5 Sl 1, p8, p2tog, p1, turn.
Row 6 Sl 1, k9, SKP, k1, turn.
Row 7 Sl 1, p10, p2tog, p1, turn.
Row 8 Sl 1, k11, SKP, k1, turn.
Row 9 Sl 1, p12, p2tog, p1, turn.
Row 10 Sl 1, k13, SKP, k1.
Row 11 Sl 1, p14, p2tog, p1, turn.
Row 12 Sl 1, k15, SKP, k1—18 sts. Cut yarn.
Next rnd (RS) With A and spare needle, pick up and k 14 sts along left side (rows) of heel (Needle 1); k30 sts of instep (Needle 2); pick up and k 14 sts along right side of heel, k9 sts from heel onto end of needle (Needle 3); sl rem 9 heel sts onto end of Needle 1—76 total sts. Rejoin yarn at beg of Needle 1.

SHAPE INSTEP
Rnd 1 Needle 1 [K1, p1] 10 times, k2tog, p1; **Needle 2** [k1, p1] 15 times; **Needle 3** k1, ssk, [k1, p1] 10 times.
Rnd 2 *P1, k1; rep from * around.
Rnd 3 Needle 1 K to last 3 sts, k2tog, k1; **Needle 2** knit; **Needle 3** k1, ssk, knit to end.
Rnd 4 Knit.
Beg with rnd 8 of chart 1, cont to foll chart 1 and shape instep working rnds 3 and 4 six times more—60 sts, AT THE SAME TIME, when chart 1 is completed, foll rows 1–22 of chart 2 once, then rows 3–19 of chart 1 once. Next rnd With MC, knit.

SHAPE TOE
Cont with MC only, work as foll:
Rnd 1 Needle 1 K to last 3 sts, k2tog, k1; **Needle 2** k1, ssk, k to last 3 sts, k2tog, k1; **Needle 3** k1, ssk, knit to end of needle.
Rnd 2 Knit. Rep last 2 rnds 7 times more—28 sts. Divide sts evenly onto 2 needles and weave toe sts tog using Kitchener st.

FINISHING
Block socks being careful not to flatten rib.

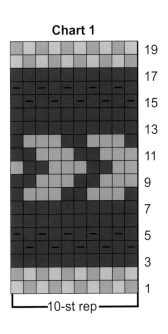

Chart 1

19
17
15
13
11
9
7
5
3
1

⌐—10-st rep—⌐

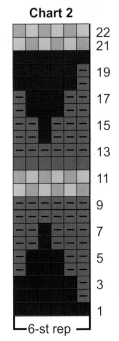

Chart 2

22
21
19
17
15
13
11
9
7
5
3
1

⌐—6-st rep—⌐

Color Key
■ Navy (MC)
■ Dark green (A)
▨ Light blue (B)
■ Denim blue (C)
▨ Light green (D)
⊟ P on RS, k on WS

BASIC RIBBED socks

Eye[4]Media, Bob Connors

You'll Need

YARN ❶
- 3½oz/100g, 480yd/440m of any cotton, wool and nylon blend fingering weight sock yarn in navy (man's), light blue (woman's), or green (child's)

NEEDLES
- One set (4) size 1 (2.25mm) double-pointed needles (dpns) *or size to obtain gauge*

OTHER MATERIALS
- Stitch markers

KNITTED MEASUREMENTS
Leg width 8 (7½, 6¼)"/20.5 (19, 16)cm
Foot length 8½ (7½, 5¼)"/21.5 (19, 13.5)cm

GAUGE
36 sts and 44 rnds to 4"/10cm over k4, p2 rib (slightly stretched) using size 1 (2.25mm) needles.
Take time to check gauge.

MAN'S SOCKS
CUFF
Cast on 64 sts loosely and divide evenly over 3 needles. Join, taking care not to twist sts. Place marker for end of rnd and sl marker every rnd. Work in k1, p1 rib for 3"/7.5cm, inc 8 sts evenly spaced across last rnd—72 sts.

LEG
Rnd 1 P1, *k4, p2; rep from * around, end k4, p1. Place a 2nd marker at center back. Rep rnd 1 for pat and work even until piece measures 6"/15cm from beg of leg.
Next rnd Work to last 23 sts of end of rnd, sl these sts and first 17 sts of rnd to 1 needle for heel, sl rem 32 sts on 2 needles for instep.

HEEL
K across 40 heel sts, dec 4 sts evenly spaced across—36 sts.
Next row (WS) Sl 1 purlwise, p to end.
Next row *Wyib sl 1 purlwise, k1; rep from * to end. Rep last 2 rows 18 times more.

TURN HEEL
Next row (WS) Sl 1, p20, p2tog, p1, turn.
Next row Sl 1, k7, ssk, k1, turn. **Next row** Sl 1, p8, p2tog, p1, turn. Cont to work towards sides of heel, having 1 more st before dec on each row until 22 sts rem.

GUSSET AND FOOT
With same needle, pick up and k 18 sts on side of heel; keeping pat as established, work 32 instep sts to Needle 2; with Needle 3, pick up and k 18 sts on other side of heel and k 11 heel sts to same needle. Place markers for end of rnd and center of sole. There are 29 sts on each of Needles 1 and 3, 32 sts on 2nd, or instep needle. Work 1 rnd even.
Next rnd K to last 3 sts of Needle 1, k2tog, k1; work even across Needle 2; on Needle 3, k1, ssk, k to end. Rep last 2 rnds 8 times more—72 sts. Work even in pat until 2"/5cm less than desired finished length.

SHAPE TOE
Discontinue pat. Beg at center of sole, place 18 sts on each of Needles 3 and 1, and 36 sts on instep needle.
Rnd 1 K to last 3 sts of Needle 1, k2tog, k1; on Needle 2, k1, ssk, k to last 3 sts, k2tog, k1; on Needle 3, k1, ssk, k to end. K 1 rnd. Rep last 2 rnds until 20 sts rem. K5 sts of Needle 1, sl on Needle 3 (sole sts).

FINISHING

Divide sts onto 2 needles and weave toe sts tog using Kitchener st. Block socks being careful not to flatten rib.

WOMAN'S SOCKS

CUFF

Cast on 66 sts loosely and divide on 3 needles. Join, taking care not to twist sts. Place marker for end of rnd and sl marker every rnd. Work in k1, p1 rib for 2"/5cm.

LEG

Rnd 1 K2, *p2, k4; rep from * around. Rep rnd 1 for pat until piece measures 3"/7.5cm from beg of leg. Work next 32 sts to 2 needles for instep, k rem 34 sts on one needle for heel, dec 2 sts evenly spaced across heel sts—32 heel sts.

HEEL

Row 1 (WS) Sl 1 purlwise, p to end.
Row 2 *Wyib sl 1 purlwise, k1; rep from * to end.
Rep last 2 rows 14 times more.

Turn heel

Next row (WS) Sl 1, p18, p2tog, p1, turn.
Next row Sl 1, k7, SSK, k1, turn.
Next row Sl 1, p8, p2tog, p1, turn.
Next row Sl 1, k9, SSK, k1, turn.
Next row Sl 1, p10, p2tog, p1, turn.
Cont to work toward sides of heel, having 1 st more before dec on each row, until 20 sts rem.

GUSSET AND FOOT

With same needle, pick up and k 16 sts on side edge of heel; with Needle 2, cont in pat on 32 instep sts; with Needle 3, pick up and k 16 sts on other side of heel, k10 heel sts to same needle. Place marker for end of rnd and center of sole (26 sts on each of Needles 1 and 3, 32 sts on 2nd, or instep needle). Work 1 rnd, in pat as established.

Next rnd K to last 3 sts of end of Needle 1, k2tog, k1; on Needle 2 work across instep sts; on Needle 3, k1, ssk, k to end. Rep last 2 rnds 9 times more—64 sts. Cont to work in pat on instep sts until 1¾"/4.5cm less than desired finished length (16 sts on each of Needles 1 and 3, 32 sts on 2nd or instep needle).

Shape Toe

Beg at center of sole, k to last 3 sts of Needle 1, k2tog, k1; on Needle 2, k1, ssk, k to last 3 sts, k2tog, k1; on Needle 3, k1, ssk, k to end. K 1 rnd. Rep last 2 rnds until 16 sts rem. K4 sts of Needle 1 and sl to Needle 3.

FINISHING

See Man's Socks Finishing.

CHILD'S SOCKS

CUFF

Cast on 56 sts loosely, divide over 3 needles. Join, taking care not to twist sts. Place marker for end of rnd and sl marker every rnd. Work in k1, p1 rib for 1½"/4cm.

LEG

Rnd 1 *K3, p1; rep from * around. Rep rnd 1 until 4"/10cm from beg of leg, end 12 sts before end of last rnd. Sl last 12 sts and first 15 sts of rnd to 1 needle for heel; sl rem 29 sts to 2 needles for instep.

HEEL

K across heel sts, dec 1 st at center.
Next row (WS) Sl first st purlwise, p to end.
Next row *Wyib sl 1 purlwise, k1; rep from * to end. Rep last 2 rows 13 times more.

Turn heel

Next row (WS) Sl 1, p14, p2tog, p1, turn.
Next row Sl 1, k5, ssk, k1, turn.
Next row Sl 1, p6, p2tog, p1, turn.
Next row Sl 1, k7, ssk, k1, turn.
Next row Sl 1, p8, p2tog, p1, turn. Cont to work towards sides of heel, having 1 st more before dec on each row, until 16 sts rem, end with a RS row.

GUSSET AND FOOT

With same needle, pick up 15 sts on side of heel, work 29 instep sts to same needle, with Needle 2, pick up and k 15 sts on other side of heel, k first 8 heel sts to same needle. Place marker for end of rnd and center of sole (23 sts on Needles 1 and 3, 29 sts on 2nd or instep needle). Work 1 rnd even, working pat over instep sts.

Next rnd K to last 3 sts of Needle 1, k2tog, k1; work pat across Needle 2; on Needle 3 k1, ssk, k to end. Rep last 2 rnds until 14 sts rem on each of Needles 1 and 3—57 sts. Work even until 1½"/4cm less than desired finished length. Discontinue pat. K 1 rnd, dec 1 st in center of Needle 2.

Shape Toe

Beg at center of sole, k to last 3 sts of Needle 1, k2tog, k1; on Needle 2, k1, ssk, k to last 3 sts, k2tog, k1; on Needle 3, k1, SSK, k to end. K 1 rnd. Rep last 2 rnds until 16 sts rem. K4 sts of Needle 1, sl on Needle 3 (sole sts).

FINISHING

See Man's Socks Finishing.

Eye[4]Media, Bob Connors

BABY socks

SIZES

Instructions are written for infant's size 3-6 months. Changes for sizes 9-12 months are in parentheses.

KNITTED MEASUREMENTS

Leg width 4½"/11.5cm
Foot length 3¼ (3¾)"/8 (9.5)cm

GAUGE

28 sts and 40 rnds/rows to 4"/10cm over chart pat using size 2 (2.75mm) needle. *Take time to check your gauge.*

SOCKS

CUFF

Beg at cuff edge, cast on 32 sts on one needle. Divide sts onto 3 needles, with 10 sts on Needle 1, 12 sts on Needle 2 and 10 sts on Needle 3. Join, taking care to not twist sts on needles. Mark end of rnd and sl marker every rnd. Work in k2, p2 rib for 5 rnds. K 2 rnds. Then beg with rnd 1 of chart for chosen style, work 8-st rep 4 times. Work through rnd 10. Then work rnds 1-9 once.

HEEL

Rnd 10 Knit sts on Needle 1, knit sts on Needle 2, k first 2 sts of Needle 3, then sl the 2 sts just worked onto end of Needle 2 and last 2 sts of Needle 1 onto beg of Needle 2—16 instep sts. Divide these sts onto 2 needles and leave to be worked later for instep. Rejoin yarn to 8 sts of Needle 3 and k these 8 sts, k8 sts of Needle 1—16 heels sts. Work back and forth in rows on the 16 heel sts only.
Row 1 (WS) Sl 1, p to end.
Row 2 Sl 1, *k1, sl 1; rep from *, end k1. Rep these 2 rows until heel measures ¾"/2cm, end with a RS row.

Turn heel

Next row (WS) P10, p2tog, p1, turn.
Row 2 Sl 1, k5, ssk, k1, turn.
Row 3 Sl 1, p6, p2tog, p1, turn.
Row 4 Sl 1, k7, ssk, k1, turn.
Row 5 Sl 1, p8, p2tog, p1, turn.
Row 6 Sl 1, k8, ssk—10 sts. Cut yarn. Sl last 5 sts of heel to spare needle and cont to pick up with same needle—8 sts from side of heel (13 sts on Needle 1); work 16 instep sts cont in chart pat, (Needle 2); pick up and k8 sts from other side of heel and k5 from first needle (13 sts on Needle 3) for a total of 42 sts.

You'll Need

YARN ❶

- 1¾oz/50g ball, 190yd/ 170m) of any fingering weight merino wool yarn in blue or peach

NEEDLES

- One set (4) size 2 (2.75mm) double pointed needles (dpns) *or size to obtain gauge*

OTHER MATERIALS

- Stitch markers

SHAPE INSTEP

Rnd 1 Knit.
Rnd 2 Needle 1 K to last 3 sts, ssk, k1; **Needle 2** work even in chart pat; **Needle 3** k1, k2tog, k to end. Rep last 2 rnds 4 times more—32 sts. Then work even in chart pat on instep sts and St st on sole sts until foot measures 3¼ (3¾)"/8 (9.5) cm from beg of heel.

SHAPE TOE

Rnd 1 Needle 1 K to last 3 sts, ssk, k1; **Needle 2** k1, k2tog, k to last 3 sts, ssk, k1, **Needle 3** k1, k2tog, k to end.
Rnd 2 Knit. Rep last 2 rnds 3 times more—16 sts. Divide sts evenly onto 2 needles and weave toe sts tog using Kitchener st.

FINISHING

Block socks being careful not to flatten rib.

Girl Version Chart

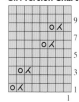

Stitch Key

▢ K on RS

⊙ Yo

⊼ K2tog

Boy Version Chart

Stitch Key

▪ K on RS

✕ Right Twist:
K2tog, k first st again, sl both sts from LH needle.

FAIR-ISLE CUFF socks

You'll Need

YARN [2]
- 1¾oz/50g, 125yd/115m; 1¾oz/50g, 125yd/115m; 3½oz/100g, 250yd/230m of any sportweight wool and and cotton blend yarn in beige (MC)
- Small amounts in dark red (A), pale blue (B), navy (C), cream (D), lilac (E) and yellow (F) in same or similar yarn

NEEDLES
- One pair each sizes 2 and 3 (2.75 and 3mm) needles *or size to obtain gauge*
- One set (4) size 3 (3mm) double-pointed needles (dpns)

OTHER MATERIALS
- Stitch holder

SIZES
Instructions are written for girl's size X-Small (4-5½). Changes for sizes Small (5-6½) and Medium (6-7½) are in parentheses.

KNITTED MEASUREMENTS
Leg width 7"/18cm
Foot length 4¾ (5½, 6½)"/12 (14, 16.5)cm

GAUGE
25 sts and 34 rows/rnds to 4"/10cm over St st using larger needles.
Take time to check your gauge.

Note When changing colors, twist yarn on WS to prevent holes.

SOCKS
CUFF
With smaller straight needles and A, cast on 49 sts. Change to MC.
Row 1 K1, *p1, k1; rep from * to end.
Row 2 P1, *k1, p1; rep from * to end.
Rep row 1 once more.
Change to larger straight needles. P 1 row.
Beg Fair Isle chart
Row 1 (RS) Work row 1 of Fair Isle chart, working 8-st rep 6 times, end with last st of chart. Cont to foll chart through row 13. **Next row (WS)** With MC, purl, dec 6 sts evenly spaced across—43 sts. Change to smaller straight needles and cont with MC only. Work in k1, p1 rib for 2¼"/6cm. Change to larger needles and beg with a k row, work 4 rows in St st. Cut yarn. Change to dpns.

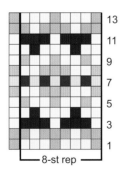

13
11
9
7
5
3
1

8-st rep

Color Key
- ☐ Beige (MC)
- ■ Dark red (A)
- ▨ Pale blue (B)
- ■ Navy (C)
- ☐ Cream (D)
- ▨ Lilac (E)
- ▨ Yellow (F)

HEEL
Sl last 10 sts of row onto one dpn, then first 9 sts of row onto same needle—19 heel sts. Work back and forth on these heel sts only. Sl rem 24 sts to a st holder for instep.
Row 1 (RS) With RS facing, join MC to 19 heel sts, k9, k2tog, k8, turn—18 sts. Work 9 rows in St st.
Turn heel
Next row (RS) K13, k2tog tbl, turn. **Next row** Sl 1, p8, p2tog, turn.

Next row Sl 1, k8, k2tog tbl, turn.
Next row Sl 1, p8, p2tog, turn.
Rep last 2 rows until there are10 sts. Cut yarn. **Next rnd** Sl first 5 sts of needle to safety pin, pm to indicate beg of rnd, join MC and k rem 5 heel sts, then pick up and k8 sts along left side (rows) of heel, k5 instep sts (Needle 1—18 sts); k 14 sts of instep (Needle 2—14 sts); k rem 5 instep sts, pick up and k 8 sts along right side (rows) of heel k5 sts from safety pin (Needle 3—18 sts)—50 total sts. Join and cont in rnds as foll:

SHAPE INSTEP
K 1 rnd. **Next rnd** K12, k2tog, k to last 14 sts, k2tog tbl, k12. K 1 rnd.
Next rnd K11, k2tog, k to last 13 sts, k2tog tbl, k11. Cont to dec in this way every other rnd having 1 less st before and after decs 3 times more—40 sts rem. Work even in St st until foot measures 3¼ (4, 5)"/8 (10, 12.5)cm from beg of heel.

SHAPE TOE
Rnd 1 [K7, k2tog, k2, k2tog tbl, k7] twice. **Rnd 2** Knit. **Rnd 3** [K6, k2tog, k2, k2tog tbl, k6] twice. **Rnd 4** Knit. Cont to dec 4 sts every other rnd in this way (repositioning sts on needles as necessary) 3 times more—20 sts rem. Divide sts evenly onto 2 needles and weave toe sts tog using Kitchener st.

FINISHING
Block socks being careful not to flatten rib. Sew leg seams, reversing Fair Isle cuff seam for cuff turnback.

KID'S STRIPED socks

You'll Need

YARN
- 3½oz/100g, 215yd/200m of any DK weight cotton yarn each in green (MC-1) or pink (MC-2) and contrast colors in purple (A), yellow, orange and blue (for both)

NEEDLES
- One set (4) each sizes 4 and 5 (3.5 and 3.75mm) double-pointed needles (dpns) *or size to obtain gauge*

KNITTED MEASUREMENTS
Leg width 6½"/16.5cm
Foot length 7¼"/18.5cm

GAUGE
22 sts and 32 rows/rnds to 4"/10cm over St st using larger dpns.
Take time to check your gauge.

Note Foll chart for chosen color way using lime (MC-1) or pink (MC-2) as the main color. Use the opposite MC color for the heel (see photo).

SOCKS
CUFF
With smaller dpn and A, loosely cast on 36 sts. Divide sts evenly on 3 needles with 12 sts on each needle. Join, taking care not to twist sts on needles. Mark end of rnd and sl marker every rnd. K 3 rnds. **Next rnd** *K2, p2; rep from * around. Cont in k2, p2 rib for 4 rnds more. Change to larger dpn. Beg with rnd 1 of stripe chart, work in St st and stripe pat using chosen colors, through rnd 40. Leg measures approx 6"/15cm from beg. Cut yarn.

HEEL
Sl first 9 sts of Needle 1 onto spare needle, then sl last 9 sts of Needle 2 onto other end of same needle—18 heel sts. Divide rem 18 sts onto 2 needles for instep to be worked later. Work back and forth in rows on the 18 heel sts only. **Row 1 (RS)** Join MC-1 (or MC-2), k18 heel sts. Cont in St st for a total of 1"/2.5cm, end with a RS row.

Turn heel
Row 1 (WS) Sl 1, p9, p2tog, p1, turn. **Row 2** Sl 1, k3, k2tog, k1, turn. **Row 3** Sl 1, p4, p2tog, p1, turn. **Row 4** Sl 1, k5, k2tog, k1, turn. **Row 5** Sl 1, p6, p2tog, p1, turn. **Row 6** Sl 1, k7, k2tog, k1—10 sts. **Row 7** Sl 1, p8, p2tog, turn. **Row 8** Sl 1, k8, k2tog, turn. Cut yarn. **Next rnd** Sl last 5 sts of heel to Needle 1 and with MC-1 or MC-2, k5, then cont with MC, pick up and k11 sts along left side (rows) of heel (16 sts—Needle 1); k next 18 sts

for instep (Needle 2); pick up and k11 sts along right side of heel, k5 from rem heel sts (16 sts—Needle 3) and a total of 50 sts. Beg with row 42, cont in stripe pat and work as foll:

SHAPE INSTEP
Rnd 1 Knit. **Rnd 2 Needle 1** K to last 3 sts, k2tog, k1; **Needle 2** knit; **Needle 3** k1, SKP, k to end. Rep last 2 rnds 6 times more—36 sts. Cont in stripe pat through rnd 79 or until foot measures 6¼"/16cm from beg of heel. Change to A.

SHAPE TOE
Rnd 1 Needle 1 K to last 3 sts, k2tog, k1; **Needle 2** k1, SKP, k to last 3 sts, k2tog, k1; **Needle 3** k1, SKP, k to end. **Rnd 2** Knit. Rep last 2 rnds 3 times more—20 sts. Divide sts evenly onto 2 needles and weave toe sts tog using Kitchener st.

FINISHING
Block socks being careful not to flatten rib.

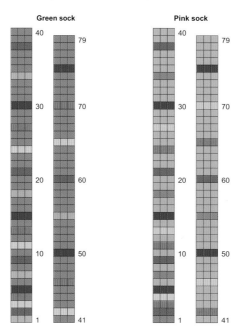

Green sock / Pink sock chart (rows 1–79, 40, 41)

Color Key
- Green
- Pink
- Blue
- Yellow
- Orange
- Purple